WITHDRAWN

MOVERS, SHAKERS, & HISTORY MAKERS

BESSIE COLEMAN
BOLD PILOT WHO GAVE WOMEN WINGS

CONTENT CONSULTANT
DOROTHY S. COCHRANE
GENERAL AVIATION CURATOR, AERONAUTICS DEPARTMENT
NATIONAL AIR AND SPACE MUSEUM

BY MARTHA LONDON

CAPSTONE PRESS
a capstone imprint

Capstone Captivate is published by Capstone Press, an imprint of Capstone.
1710 Roe Crest Drive
North Mankato, Minnesota 56003
www.capstonepub.com

Library of Congress Cataloging-in-Publication Data
Names: London, Martha, author.
Title: Bessie Coleman : bold pilot who gave women wings / Martha London.
Description: North Mankato, Minnesota : Capstone Press, 2021. | Series:
  Movers, shakers, and history makers | Includes index. | Audience: Grades
  4-6
Identifiers: LCCN 2020000940 (print) | LCCN 2020000941 (ebook) | ISBN
  9781496684769 (hardcover) | ISBN 9781496688187 (paperback) | ISBN
  9781496684967 (pdf)
Subjects: LCSH: Coleman, Bessie, 1896-1926—Juvenile literature. | African
  American women air pilots—Biography—Juvenile literature. | Air
  pilots--United States—Biography—Juvenile literature.
Classification: LCC TL540.C546 L66 2021 (print) | LCC TL540.C546 (ebook)
  | DDC 629.13092 [B]—dc23
LC record available at https://lccn.loc.gov/2020000940
LC ebook record available at https://lccn.loc.gov/2020000941

Image Credits
Alamy: Everett Collection Historical, 36, Historic Images, 19, Science History Images, 33, 38; CMG Worldwide: cover (foreground), 5, 30, 43; Getty Images: Fotosearch/Archive Photos, 29, Gordon Coster/The LIFE Picture Collection, 21, Hulton Archive, 25, Michael Ochs Archives, 26; iStockphoto: ilbusca, 14; Library of Congress: Harris & Ewing, 17, Jack Delano/Farm Security Administration - Office of War Information Photograph Collection, 7, 9; Red Line Editorial: 13, 40; Shutterstock Images: djgis, cover (background), 1, Everett Historical, 10, Kletr, 31, Roland Ijdema, 35

Editorial Credits
Editor: Charly Haley; Designer: Colleen McLaren

All internet sites appearing in back matter were available and accurate when this book was sent to press.

Printed in the United States of America.
PA117

CONTENTS

Words in **bold** are in the glossary.

CHAPTER ONE

SEEKING ADVENTURE

The plane flew through the sky. It looped in the air. The crowd gasped. It was the 1920s, and very few people had seen a plane do a loop. The motor roared as the pilot flew the plane close to the stands where the crowd sat. Black people and white people sat next to each other. They cheered for the pilot's fearlessness.

A black woman sat in the cockpit. Goggles covered her eyes. She wore a leather helmet. Bessie Coleman smiled at the audience. She was the first black woman to get her pilot's license. Her determination inspired many people, especially other black women.

Bessie Coleman amazed people with her airplane flying feats.

MAKING ENDS MEET

Elizabeth Coleman was born on January 26, 1892. Everyone called her Bessie. She was born in Atlanta, Texas. Coleman was the 10th of 13 children in her family. Her mother, Susan, was black. Her father, George, was part black and part American Indian.

Throughout the first half of the 1900s, black and white people were separated by law in the southern United States. This was called **segregation**. White and black people used different water fountains and bathrooms. They went to different schools.

And the places for black people were worse than those for white people. Black schools received less money than white schools. Black people could only sit in the backs of buses. Separating people based on race was a result of **discrimination**.

Not long after Bessie was born, her family moved to Waxahachie, Texas. Both of Bessie's parents worked as **sharecroppers**. Sharecroppers rented small areas of land to plant and harvest crops.

Many sharecroppers were black. The landowners were usually white. The landowners took some of the crops as payment. Sometimes they also made sharecroppers pay to use their tools. It was difficult for sharecroppers to earn enough money to support their families.

In the time of segregation in the south, places were labeled by race to show who was allowed to be there.

To make more money for the family, Bessie's mother also worked as a maid. She washed white people's laundry for them. When Bessie was old enough, she helped her mother with this work.

Black people and American Indian people faced violence due to **racism**. In 1901, Bessie's parents split up. Her father moved to an area in Oklahoma where American Indians had more rights than in Texas. But Bessie's mother chose not to move because she wanted to keep her job and earn money for herself and her children. She and the children stayed in Waxahachie.

Bessie's mother encouraged Bessie to succeed in school and to educate herself. Bessie loved to read. She checked out books from the traveling library.

FACT

As a child, Bessie walked 4 miles (6 kilometers) to a one-room schoolhouse each school day.

Working as maids for white people, like Bessie's mom did, was one of the only ways black women could make a living at that time.

Waxahachie did not have a permanent library. Instead a librarian traveled with a cart. The cart was filled with books. It was pulled by a mule or horse. The traveling library came to Waxahachie two or three times a year.

Black schools worked hard to educate their children with the resources they had.

LOOKING AHEAD

Bessie was seven years old when her father moved to Oklahoma. Her older siblings lived on their own. It was difficult for Bessie and her mother to pay the bills and support Bessie's younger siblings alone. They had to work hard.

Bessie's mother worked two jobs. When Bessie was not in school, she worked with her mother. She picked cotton and washed clothes. Some of the money Bessie earned went to her family. But she also saved some of it. Bessie knew she did not want to stay in Waxahachie. She saved money so she could eventually move away.

BLACK SCHOOLS AND WHITE SCHOOLS

Bessie went to school with other black children because of segregation. Schools for black children did not receive enough money from the government. They often did not have enough books or pencils for students. But black students continued to work hard for their education.

Bessie graduated from high school. She was accepted into college. At age 18, she had enough money to leave Waxahachie. She moved to Langston, Oklahoma. Bessie spent one semester at the Oklahoma Colored Agricultural and Normal University, which is now known as Langston University.

Unfortunately, Bessie was not able to continue going to school. She didn't have enough money to pay for **tuition**.

A NEW PLAN

Without any money, Coleman could not stay in Oklahoma. She moved back to Waxahachie to live with her mother and younger siblings.

FACT

It was a big deal for Bessie to get into college. Most Americans did not go to college in 1910.

Langston, Oklahoma (college)

Waxahachie, Texas (childhood)

Atlanta, Texas (born)

Coleman joined two of her older brothers in Chicago in 1915.

Coleman continued to work. She did the same things she did as a child. She washed laundry with her mother. She harvested cotton. She saved some of her money. Coleman was making plans. She knew she would not live in Waxahachie forever.

When Coleman was 23, she finally had enough money to leave home again. Two of her older brothers lived in Chicago, Illinois. They offered to let her stay with them.

Coleman packed her bags. She was not sure what the future held. But she was excited about the next adventure.

CHAPTER TWO

FINDING HER PLACE

Coleman arrived in Chicago in 1915. She moved in with her brothers. She was not sure what she wanted for a career. But Coleman enrolled in beauty school.

Coleman got a job as a manicurist. She painted people's nails. She kept saving money. To save even more money, she took another job as a manager at a restaurant. Coleman worked hard. But her life was not all work. She enjoyed living with her brothers. They told her stories about their lives away from Texas.

FARAWAY LANDS

The United States entered World War I in 1917, while Coleman was living in Chicago. Both of her brothers fought in the war. They were stationed in France. Coleman's brothers saw differences in how Americans and French people lived.

Coleman had many jobs, including working as a manicurist, to try to save money.

Women had more rights in France than in the United States. At that time in the United States, women still could not vote in elections. This did not change until 1920.

Coleman's brothers told her that French women were allowed to be pilots. Coleman was amazed. She wanted to fly too. Coleman decided she was going to become a pilot. She did not want to be a manicurist for the rest of her life.

Not many pilots were women in the early 1900s, and no female pilots were black. Most American pilots were white and wealthy. They had money to get pilot's licenses. Flying was still a new technology. Airplanes and flight classes were expensive.

FRENCH WOMEN IN FLIGHT

Women in France were allowed to fly before women in the United States. Women such as Thérèse Peltier and Raymonde de Laroche were leaders among French female pilots. Women did not fly in World War I. They flew for fun. Women set several records in the early 1900s for the longest flights.

Thérèse Peltier (right) of France is believed to be the first woman to ever fly an airplane. She first flew in 1908.

Coleman was a black woman from a poor family. She worked multiple jobs. Despite these obstacles, Coleman was determined. She began contacting flight schools in the United States.

But the United States was not ready for a black woman pilot. White people ran the American flight schools. Every flight school turned Coleman away. Many people believed women could not be pilots. Lots of white people also believed black people were not as smart as white people. These people were wrong. But that did not stop them from discriminating against Coleman and other black people.

ROBERT ABBOTT

Robert Abbott owned the *Chicago Defender*. The *Defender* was a black newspaper. It reported news about black people in the city. The major city newspapers were owned by white people. They often did not report on African American issues in Chicago. Abbott was one of the first black millionaires in the United States.

Coleman's friend, newspaper publisher Robert Abbott (right),
supported her dream of becoming a pilot.

COLEMAN AND THE FEMALE PILOTS BEFORE HER

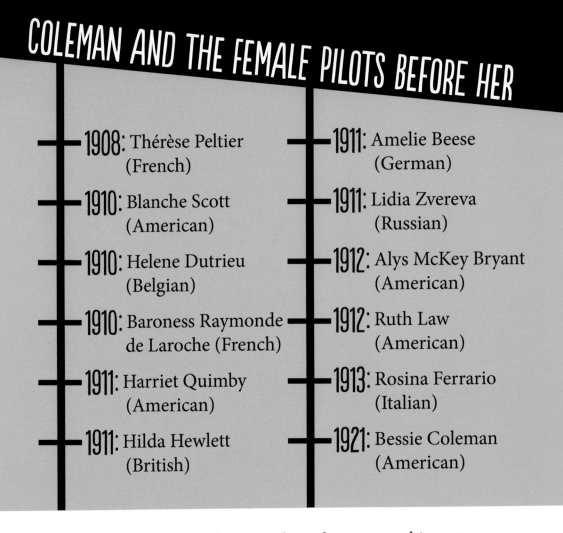

- **1908**: Thérèse Peltier (French)
- **1910**: Blanche Scott (American)
- **1910**: Helene Dutrieu (Belgian)
- **1910**: Baroness Raymonde de Laroche (French)
- **1911**: Harriet Quimby (American)
- **1911**: Hilda Hewlett (British)
- **1911**: Amelie Beese (German)
- **1911**: Lidia Zvereva (Russian)
- **1912**: Alys McKey Bryant (American)
- **1912**: Ruth Law (American)
- **1913**: Rosina Ferrario (Italian)
- **1921**: Bessie Coleman (American)

Abbott met Coleman when she was working at a barbershop. Abbott and Coleman became long-time friends. He told Coleman to get her pilot's license in France. Coleman took his advice. She decided to study in France. The only problem was Coleman did not know French. The application to the pilot's school had to be in French.

She started taking French classes at the Berlitz school in Chicago. Coleman worked two jobs during the day. In the evening, she learned French. In 1920, Coleman finished her French classes. She packed a suitcase. Coleman took all the money she had saved. She hoped it would be enough. Coleman tucked her application in her suitcase and bought a ticket to travel to France on a ship. The rest of Coleman's life waited for her across the Atlantic Ocean.

FACT

Coleman traveled to France on a ship that left from New York. It took approximately seven days to get from New York to France in 1920.

CHAPTER THREE

QUEEN BESS

Not long after Coleman arrived in France, her application was accepted, and she enrolled in an **aviation** school. Coleman did not know anything about airplanes or flying. But she was ready to learn.

ON A BIPLANE

The school's plane was an old biplane. A biplane had two sets of wings. In the early years, planes were made of wood and canvas. This allowed the planes to be lighter. But these early planes were also more fragile. The biplanes were known to break apart when pilots turned too sharply.

The school's biplane broke down regularly. Sometimes it stopped working in midair. Coleman and other students had to learn how to get the plane started again. Coleman learned to stay calm.

Coleman attended the Caudron Brothers' School of Aviation in France. The Caudron brothers also designed new aircraft such as this biplane.

Coleman learned to fly biplanes at aviation school.
Flying these planes was dangerous.

But accidents did happen. Not all of Coleman's classmates survived the training. Airplanes were not as safe back then as they are today. The cockpits were not enclosed, and there were no seat belts. This meant pilots could fall out of the cockpits. Even though Coleman was sad when there was an accident, she was determined to be a pilot. She worked hard and tried to stay safe during her lessons.

GRADUATION

Less than a year after arriving in France, Coleman graduated from flight school. Her graduation was a major milestone. She was the first black and American Indian woman to get a pilot's license and the first American woman to graduate from a French flight school. Coleman hoped people in the United States would recognize her accomplishments.

Coleman headed back to the United States with her international pilot's license. Coleman had big dreams. She wanted to start her own aviation school. She did not want other people to experience the discrimination she faced. If she had her own school, more women and people of color could become pilots.

But Coleman needed money to do that. She had used up her savings in France. Before she could start a school, she needed to find a way to earn money as a pilot.

STUNT PILOT

Commercial flights were not common in the 1920s. Planes were still small. They could only fit two people. One way to earn money by flying was to become a **stunt** pilot. Stunt pilots performed tricks in the air for entertainment. They were fearless.

FACT

Stunt pilots were sometimes called barnstormers. They toured through rural areas performing shows.

Coleman knew she could be a stunt pilot. But she needed more training. She looked for schools in the United States to teach her. But the American flight schools still did not want to teach a black woman. No one wanted to teach Coleman even though she had a pilot's license already.

Coleman decided to go back to France. She went to the flight school where she had studied before. Her teachers taught her more skills. After less than a year, Coleman was ready to return to the United States.

Once Coleman became a pilot, she worked to help other women and people of color learn to fly too.

As a black woman, Coleman (front, left) had to work even harder for the chance to attend flight school.

People in France noticed Coleman's amazing flying skills. News of her skills spread. Soon people were excited about her return to the United States. Some people in France said she was the best pilot in the world. Reporters greeted Coleman when she returned to the United States. Newspaper reporters interviewed her. Even white news companies wanted to learn about Coleman. She was ready to make a name for herself.

COLEMAN'S PLANE

Coleman flew different airplanes, but most often she flew the JN-4 "Jenny" biplane.

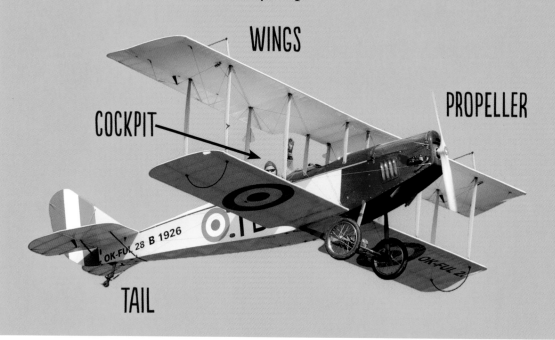

WINGS

PROPELLER

COCKPIT

TAIL

IN BUSINESS

In 1922, Coleman performed her first flight show. Robert Abbott, who owned the *Chicago Defender*, helped arrange the **exhibition** in New York City. Then Coleman went back to Chicago. She performed another air show. More people in the United States were beginning to notice her.

Coleman wanted to keep performing. It would be easier if she had her own airplane, but she did not have enough money to buy one. She had to borrow planes. Many of the planes she used were old World War I planes. Some were not reliable. But Coleman performed in any airplane she could get.

FACT

Coleman sometimes left the cockpit and walked on the wings of her plane while flying.

Audiences loved Coleman's shows. She was known for her loop-the-loops and figure eights. People had not seen pilots do what Coleman was doing. Most female performers at the time only walked on airplane wings. Very few actually flew the planes. She tried new things in her planes. People gasped when she did a dangerous stunt. They cheered when she succeeded.

People nicknamed Coleman "Brave Bessie" and "Queen Bess" for her skills. Coleman was finding success. But she was not going to stop and relax. Coleman wanted to make a difference in the world.

People were shocked by Coleman's skill and bravery as a stunt pilot.

CHAPTER FOUR

STANDING UP FOR RIGHTS

It was not easy being a stunt pilot. Coleman had to work hard. Not all of the air shows were well attended. She was paid little money for some of the performances. Some of the show managers offered segregated shows. But Coleman refused to perform at shows that separated black people and white people.

CIVIL RIGHTS

At exhibitions, many shows made black people enter through a separate gate. Black people had to sit in a different part of the stands than white people. Coleman did not want that. She was an **advocate** for civil rights.

Coleman's daring stunts continue to inspire pilots to take risks during their shows.

Coleman was among many black Americans who spoke out against segregation. These protests continued for years, into the 1960s.

Coleman told show managers she would not perform for segregated crowds. Every person had to enter through one gate. At the time, it was a radical request. Few public spaces allowed white people and black people to interact with one another, especially in southern states.

For Coleman, being a pilot was fun. But she did not just want to fly. Coleman tried to inspire people. She wanted other people to become excited about aviation.

TEACHING OTHERS

Coleman began giving lectures and showing films to teach people about flying. This helped Coleman make more money. She wanted to buy her own plane.

Coleman toured schools and churches. She focused on schools for black children. Coleman especially loved talking to girls. Many girls at this time had probably not seen a woman pilot before. Coleman wanted every girl to know that she could reach her dreams.

Coleman gave speeches about how she became a pilot. She also showed films of her performing stunts. Few students had seen a stunt pilot perform live. Coleman's lectures provided a way to bring her show to the children.

HER OWN PLANE

Coleman continued giving lectures and performing in air shows. Black newspapers published articles about Coleman's flying career. This helped Coleman get more jobs. She finally had enough money to buy her own plane in 1923. But her new plane was difficult to fly. She ended up crashing it. Coleman broke her leg and several ribs. She had to take more than a year off from flying. She recovered in Chicago. After her broken leg healed, Coleman got back to work. Crowds were waiting for her.

Coleman made a career out of her air show performances and speeches.

But after so many months away from working, Coleman did not have any money to replace her wrecked plane. In 1926, Coleman asked a wealthy businessman to sponsor her. He gave Coleman the money to buy another plane.

The plane was old. But Coleman had a mechanic she trusted. They could make it work. In 1926, Coleman and her mechanic, William Wills, went to Jacksonville, Florida, for an air show. Coleman arrived before Wills. Wills flew the plane from Dallas, Texas, to Jacksonville. On the flight from Texas to Florida, Wills had to make several emergency landings. The engine was acting up.

NATIONAL AVIATION HALL OF FAME

Coleman was inducted into the National Aviation Hall of Fame in 2006. This organization honors American aviators. Others in the hall of fame include Wilbur and Orville Wright, who built the first successful airplane, and Neil Armstrong, the first man to walk on the moon.

DELIVERING COLEMAN'S PLANE

Mechanic William Wills flew from Dallas to Jacksonville to bring Coleman's airplane to her. He had to make many repairs along the way.

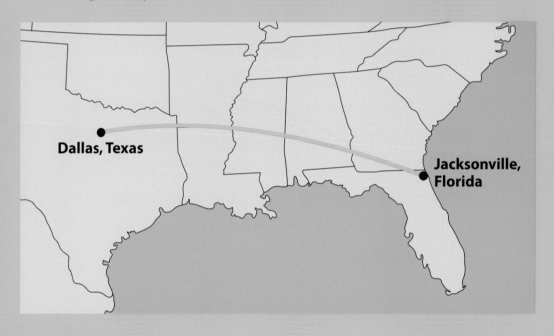

Dallas, Texas

Jacksonville, Florida

AN ACCIDENT

Wills got to Jacksonville safely. He finished a few repairs on the plane. Then Wills and Coleman decided to practice for a performance that was scheduled for the next day.

Wills flew the plane. Coleman was in the rear cockpit. She was going to parachute out of the plane during the show. Coleman was looking for the best place to jump out. She was not wearing her seat belt. She needed to lean over the side of the plane to get a good look at her surroundings.

A loose wrench was on the floor of the cockpit. It slid forward. The wrench jammed the engine. Wills lost control of the aircraft. Coleman fell out of the plane and died. Wills also died when the plane crashed. Coleman was 34, and Wills was 24.

A LEGACY

Three memorial services were held for Coleman. One was in Jacksonville and another was in Orlando, Florida. People in Florida wanted to honor Coleman where she died. The third memorial was in Chicago.

FACT

Approximately 5,000 people attended Coleman's memorial in Orlando. In Chicago, 15,000 people went to Coleman's memorial service.

Ida B. Wells read an essay at the memorial service in Chicago. She recognized the important work Coleman did for racial equality. Like Coleman, Wells was an advocate for civil rights. She was a famous black reporter of the early 1900s.

People around the United States were sad to hear of Coleman's death. People knew being a pilot was a dangerous career. But Coleman was one of the best. Even after her death, Coleman continued to inspire people.

Many people credit Coleman with the formation of famous aviation groups. For example, the Blackbirds was a group of black stunt pilots in the 1930s. The Blackbirds flew in patterns as a group. In the 1970s, a group of black women pilots founded the Bessie Coleman Aviators Club.

BECAUSE OF BESSIE

William J. Powell was a black business owner in Chicago. He was inspired by Coleman. In 1929, he founded the Bessie Coleman Aero Club in Los Angeles, California, to teach black men and women to fly.

The Bessie Coleman Aero Club was created to carry out Coleman's legacy.

The United States became less segregated in the years after Coleman's death. Specific laws that made segregation legal in southern states were finally stopped in the 1960s. Even though Coleman did not live to see that happen, her work had an effect on it. Today, Coleman remains an important figure in civil rights history.

TIMELINE

1892: Bessie Coleman is born in Atlanta, Texas.

1901: Coleman's father moves to Oklahoma. Coleman, her mother, and her siblings stay in Texas.

1910: Coleman moves to Langston, Oklahoma, for college. But she is unable to pay for school and moves back to Texas after less than a year.

1915: Coleman moves to Chicago to live with her brothers.

1920: Coleman moves to France to study aviation.

1921: Coleman earns her pilot's license.

1922: Coleman performs her first flight show in New York City.

1923: Coleman buys her own airplane. The plane is later destroyed in a crash.

1926: A businessman helps Coleman buy another plane.

1926: Coleman dies in a plane crash while practicing for an air show.

2006: Many years after her death, Coleman is inducted into the National Aviation Hall of Fame.

GLOSSARY

advocate (AD-vuh-kuht)
a person who supports a cause

aviation (AY-vee-ay-shun)
having to do with flight

discrimination (dis-kri-muh-NAY-shuhn)
when a person is treated unfairly because of a trait, such as race or gender

exhibition (ek-suh-BI-shuhn)
a performance to demonstrate a skill for a crowd

racism (RAY-siz-uhm)
when people are treated unfairly because of the color of their skin

segregation (seg-ruh-GAY-shuhn)
separation by race

sharecroppers (SHAIR-krop-urz)
people who rent land to farm

stunt (STUHNT)
a trick performed for a crowd

tuition (too-IH-shun)
the cost to attend a college or university

READ MORE

Baker, Brynn. *Tuskegee Airmen: Freedom Flyers of World War II*. North Mankato, MN: Capstone Press, 2016.

Downs, Mike. *Invention of Flight*. Vero Beach, FL: Rourke Educational Media, 2020.

Head, Deirdre R.J. *Dorothy Vaughan*. North Mankato, MN: Capstone Press, 2021.

INTERNET SITES

National Aviation Hall of Fame: Bessie Coleman
https://www.nationalaviation.org/our-enshrinees/coleman-bessie/

National Women's History Museum: Bessie Coleman
https://www.womenshistory.org/education-resources/biographies/bessie-coleman

Smithsonian National Air and Space Museum: Bessie Coleman
https://airandspace.si.edu/explore-and-learn/topics/women-in-aviation/coleman.cfm

INDEX